New Women's Voices Series 2017 Winner

BETWEEN

New Women's Voices Series, No. 141

poems by

Kimberly Quiogue Andrews

Finishing Line Press
Georgetown, Kentucky

BETWEEN

New Women's Voices Series, No. 141

Copyright © 2018 by Kimberly Quiogue Andrews
ISBN 978-1-63534-507-0 First Edition
All rights reserved under International and Pan-American Copyright Conventions. No part of this book may be reproduced in any manner whatsoever without written permission from the publisher, except in the case of brief quotations embodied in critical articles and reviews.

ACKNOWLEDGMENTS

Grateful acknowledgement is made to the editors and readers of the publications in which some of these poems have appeared:

"She said between" Parts 1 & 2 appeared in *The Recluse*
"The universe isn't particularly concerned"; "Fixing the world is a matter of both drastic and incremental measures," and "The bass line to Ciaran Lavery's "A Ragtime Song" is almost identical to that of Ani DiFranco's "Pulse," she finds out at thirty-three" appeared in *Muse/A*
"But don't you think we already have enough meterology, she said" appeared in *The Mackinac*
"Over the past few days of growth and destruction" appeared in *The Shallow Ends*
"She said between" Parts 3 & 4 appeared in *EOAGH*.

I thank Leah Maines for plucking this book out of the pile and selecting it as the winner of the New Women's Voices Prize for Poetry. I thank Rachel Mennies for her unwavering support of my work and my person; Daniel Story for looking over some real early drafts of these poems; Erik Freer for packaging it miraculously; and Rachel Engel both for the photo on the back and for being in so many of my thoughts as this was being written. We can't save everyone.

Publisher: Leah Maines
Editor: Christen Kincaid
Cover Art and Design: Erik Freer
Author Photo: Rachel Engel

Printed in the USA on acid-free paper.
Order online: www.finishinglinepress.com
also available on amazon.com

Author inquiries and mail orders:
Finishing Line Press
P. O. Box 1626
Georgetown, Kentucky 40324
U. S. A.

Table of Contents

1	The universe isn't particularly concerned
2	Some notes on the glass of the metropolis
3	Inattention
4	She said *between* Part 1
5	"Fixing the world is a matter of both drastic and incremental measures"
6	If there were flight, I'd eliminate the snow
8	Over the past few days of growth and destruction
9	More wings, this time of various species
11	She said *between* Part 2
12	Almost mum season; you can tell by the length of the days
13	Love in a time of neglected tropical diseases
15	The English garden
16	Elegy for x, or, it's a pity she doesn't know more about physics
17	To open the mouth is to experience pain
18	She said *between* Part 3
19	The bass line to Ciaran Lavery's "A Ragtime Song" is almost identical to that of Ani DiFranco's "Pulse," she finds out at thirty-three
20	I'll try to be less attentive to the voices, she said
21	Four-four, or, it's possible we make music because we are herd animals
23	So what if everything's planted in neat rows?
24	But don't you think we already have enough meteorology, she said
25	She said *between* Part 4
26	Favor: cleaning out the garage
27	I wanted to write about cooking, she said, but then I realized
29	Sometimes, she thinks she prefers him on the other side of the screen
30	Either pro or against Corinthians
32	Notes

For the birds and the bees

The universe isn't particularly concerned

...on the contrary, it doesn't even bother to fill in
the remainder of the test sheet. But we go on thinking
about the specificities. A cedar waxwing punctuates
a bush, the hard berry in its beak reminiscent
of difficulty, of our last meal. And everything sticks
out from this world in such a way that we are become
a spiny chestnut hull, bristling against the fire
that makes us sweet. Again, it's small, edible things
that help bring us into focus. The waxwing swallows
the berry whole, we make gestures about nourishment
and too many birds in too many poems. The continuing
cold makes us tear up, reddens the nose and the cheeks,
a reminder that there is almost nothing, at any
point, separating what's inside from what's out.
The other day I had to make a decision between two trees—
and couldn't, for fear that both were rising from the ground
in escape, that both were an essential spine. This time
I mean the bones which make us human. As much as
we skirt the subject, the language we conjure from
the very base of our skulls shrivels to a fine powder
as we throw it into the air, in celebration or in grief.
All these little collisions which throw off the light
of being destroyed. We chew up the leaves and feathers
and spit out the changeable space between molecules—
the berry, the branch, the scaly embrace.

Some notes on the glass of the metropolis

A tumbler, heavy-bottomed, a shot in the dark—
as in, *kapow!* on glass, under stars, the waxing moon

and its variable hors d'oeuvres—the evening through
a sweating drink. The on, the off, the way in which
the frame opens its mouth, gathers breath—

*take the brick on either side of the window and fill
it with arms, some hair, the flesh of a body
you imagine to be desperately, violently obsessed* (don't

forget the list you've made of each overused
term for *want*). A floor lamp is more successful
than your shoulders. I'd thought about describing

the speed of the clouds across the sky but then
again the human ability to comprehend numbers
remains poor. Void of temporal reference. You can't

tell in space anyways, who keeps track of sixteen
sunrises a day? —you'd feel old, seeing so many dawns.
This light, composed from street-level in trapezoids

of ceiling, of plaster, drop tile, parquet, tin,
the empty second sky

in its various textures, almost-heads of almost-
halos. Almost motion. I'm developing a crick

in the neck of my vowels. I'm putting my hands
against my lower back, oh, ah, the stranger's bed,
dissolving in a ring of salt.

The greed of discovery makes a mouth
out of the point of each pelvic bone. The expanse,
the fixtures filled with insects fried by instinct.

In this city of Icarus, I would stare into the sun
until the hills of my face became a lake of wax.

Inattention

The forgetting
about pockets and the laundering
of small, used up things.
I jot down:

Milk.
Paper napkins.
A sense of accomplishment.
Being and Time.
Raspberries.
~~*I am incapable of being alone.*~~ *The capacity to be alone.*
Plastic forks.

It is the time of year wherein
we are scolded by mother robins. And
there's something else singing his heart out
in that other tree. Abandon,
                        I mean,
really, what a word. Both *I leave you*
and *I love you.* All those hollows. The temperature
change at night has been drastic.
The sun corroborates me.
In the dark, we cling to each other
in almost-surprise,
                    almost-want,
garments around an agitator
pulling the coins from our hands
as we move towards a blank cleanliness,
spun and sodden.

She said *between* Part 1

What's the use of going on about
the linking of flesh to flesh when
one's own *habitus* wanders around
muttering to itself "today you will
not raise your hand but tomorrow
you will see around your head a
coronet of deer in the fields
both safe and in danger
simultaneously"

I have no reason to be called
an angel when I walk outside
I have taken the recommended
pills to make myself a chimney
I have stopped taking these to
make myself a vase in expectation

In the town square
there are many ways of crossing
without setting foot on the grass
courthouse church library
church church Catholic church
Dunkin Donuts Edible Arrangements

To the extent that the pull of skin
around the chest indicates decorum
there will be men holding flowers
and women holding flowers
and everyone else peels an apple
knowing that allegiance is a luxury
the center-justification of
this poem is a luxury
hey do you get it // do you get it

"Fixing the world is a matter of both dramatic and incremental measures"

What if we were bigger or smaller than the we thought we were. What if in the patterns of a woven rug there were streets, the lineated confluence that from above looks a bit like a llama designating a marketplace in which each strand of wool is a pillar holding up tiny fruits. We might then ask ourselves who lives here, who buys (do they buy) the micron pomegranates and brings them home (do they home) to split them, beat their nano seeds into a waiting bowl with the back of a wooden spoon. We might wonder if the pomegranates come from the red part of the carpet, the part that is pomegranate-colored, the part of every rug that is pomegranate-colored. If we are smaller than we thought we were, we tend to our lemon trees. The shadows crossing us are reconciled as vapor without instinct. If we are bigger, perhaps we sweep across the rich mazes of the rug with the tip of a violin bow, shifting the patterns ever so slightly one way, then ever so slightly the other. Perhaps this looks like movement or the desire for movement. Whether it is felt as a breeze or hurricane is a function of our ability to interpret what we cannot know. Our ability to gauge the circumference of the combined sum of what we can hold, what we could shake into nothing but choose not to.

If there were flight, I'd eliminate the snow

For years the only book
I lent out was a horror story
in seven parts, which made it easier
to get accustomed to the idea
of relinquishing
(it's only monsters,
it's not like I'm going to forget
the part where a character,
some woman,
fucks a demon so that the protagonist,
some man,
can go on shooting)—
we leave nothing but pellets
full of tiny bones—
don't tell me
about the changes in person,
about your confusion in front of a
crowd, this series of t-shirts,
or hats—
what am I doing such that
you can get on with your life,
such that I am a comfortable
red idea or the slope
down which
you can slide, over and over
again like a child
on a sled on a snow day
that's nothing but play—
something about rising out of the bed
like a phoenix
[I scribble it out]
or beginning with the tree
inquiring at the window, some
hooked mouth in the branches,
something spreading
through the darkness—
come over,
my hands have forgotten

how to touch you without shame,
I have given away
my entire library, you've
borrowed all these hollows,
my fingers are beaks
clamped into the flesh of what I
have caught by surprise,
what I let go of
too late for it to live.

Over the past few days of growth and destruction

the creeks have picked up speed, merging on to warmer highways

a bit of the air above my head has recognized the advent of a new month and pauses

every moment has seemed long and brave, an overwintered carrot

I've come to think of length and bravery as the crumpled event of a kite crashing into a tree

you've receded, in opposition to the season's flinging of blue china plates

help has not come, the incomprehensible song of the early crocus

my arms in their grasping have formed room after room, a clicking series of hinges

each unfinished sentence has furnished this new and difficult house

the neighborhood of your outline, paling silhouette, has pasted itself to my door

More wings, this time of various species

I.
For every cellular movement, there is a moment of insanity
during which synthesis seems possible—I mean
the way in which grass offsets the sunset,

then after a brief pause, bends down wetly in the morning
and you'd swear that it was a lover, their multiplicities
picking something up off of the floor—

this collective thing. Don't worry about all the people
in the room, their skeletons hinging in the dark,
and anyway, what I'm after is the changeability

of leaves in their turning, the unsung enormity of stepping
through a doorway into the mild world,
the curvature of neck into shoulder,

the plateau of us, our horizontal movements (when
we're not lying down, when everything isn't
reversed). I said *you panic*,

thrashing about like a bat in an attic.

II.
In order to compare comparisons, I need only to say that
a comparison is *like*, perhaps, a series of small objects
placed on a wooden railing.

That when I do not designate—*this one and this one and
the one before*—all sex becomes a mouthful
of chrysanthemum flowers. Upon

waking, there are my toes, their little way with little bones.
The crow's rough cough at that point
allows us to assume

that we will wish the day had neglected us, or maybe
I presume, maybe my legs are not
the adjacent library,

maybe my life is literally toast (with proffered espresso).
Do not underestimate me. I know night
when I see it. No matter who

you are, your hair is dark at the nape of your neck.

She said *between* Part 2

clap together the rings
which vee between the knuckles

that lead in a well-formed punch

what you are clocking is your thighs
meager and metallic thinking

this is not what I mean by *convergence*

this is not what I mean when I say
I am a woman because in fact

what I mean is that the landscape

rushing by the window
turns me into a mild parchment

into birch bark in its loose embrace

to practice in the mirror
I am a man / I am a man / I am a

to sit in the tub full of pennies and take

them into yourself as blood medicine
arteries hardening in greenbronze

fists curling around a note

carved into a pale stem which reads
today you may do as you wish

Almost mum season; you can tell by the length of the days

The way the sparrows populate the nearest sycamore
is of a weight being held, but absentmindedly,

as in shoes, or a fall coat. The way the dahlias at
the weekly market bend from their containers

is of the weight of pigment, sodden and overfull
of beauty upon which it is useless to comment—

instead, wedding bouquets. Regiments of lilies,
roses arranged in an airless dome. The sterile

roosting of selfsame birds and their brainless
twittering. Isn't it lovely, the clear day, the variegated

trunk, the light in its angles across the swept
floor? Are the chairs not at attention? Are the kiwis

not green and tart and full of seeds? I do not know
how to divide my life. The smell of the hay

and the sea, wishing my own husband were
a bowl of pebbles on the windowsill. Understand

that the need to bundle the flowers so tightly is
in fact the florist's kindness: something substantial

in the panicked hand, something that can be squeezed
hard and maintain its shape against recognition.

Love in a time of neglected tropical diseases

Things not to make poetry out of:

The public health worker I once married

Infrastructural issues

The ramifications of decreased public funding for public goods

Drac — unc — uliasis? Draconian uncles

You see the problem

You usher me into river blindness

You alert me to leishmaniasis

***

To go limp in front of enormity is a specialty of mine
despite the constant barking of knowing-better floating up
through the department stairwell—
                                        For now, what if

a lot of exclamation marks sufficed:
                              What!!!
                              The!!!
                              Fuck!!!

To shield your face from the sun you wind up saluting it

Shoving a stick into a puddle creates two sticks due to physics

Affect is an extreme sensitivity to time   space
continuous   I'm sorry

To make a heart with the hands: push
the first fingers together like rams and the thumbs
also with their own pulses together—
                                      the fact of the finger pulse
the heart in the finger

the heart	what luck that it beats
the finger	what luck that it beats
the stick	demand better for the ill, demand active repair, demand the elimination of the words clogging the space behind our unduly strong teeth

***

your legs, crooked, in the dark of the windowless night

The English garden

useless and cruel, the pathetic fallacy—

the pheasants that appear in the yard, the wind
bowing the darkening branches to tell us
that death is the pebble and the carriageway

the tools in the garage and the remaining dog's
small, damp footprints on the tile

could we feel otherwise

the weather moves through the hair
like a comb dipped in wine—

unable to wait, you dig the grave in the dark,
and I say *the grave*
the multiple meanings

of bed
pushing up the daisies this is the incorrect time

the motions of bending
and throwing have their meanings in relation to the cold

it takes a very long time

the night shift asks why we don't come
to a mutual understanding of all this

the headlight bobs in space

I watch from the table at the window

I'm sorry, I think, that you are full of voles

Elegy for x, or, it's a pity she does not know more about physics

I.
And what do the lobes of the leaves say
about health?
          In the afternoon, I become
fastidious, my hands like mothers checking
on each thing, reaffirming the curtains,
the coasters, the grapefruit in its place
on the counter.
          Not a thing moves, not
one threatens the door.
          The floors
in my house are radically uneven; my
possessions seek out corners and wait
there, swords in hand. Each light translates
differently in each room.

II.
Nighttime and its contradictions: stillness
amplified, yet small motions also amplified.
The rustling of sheets; one cricket's leg
against another—
          What I am trying to say
is that permanence is a black wave
on some blinking sea.
          Does my
interlocutor lament me? Do I dare
proclaim another thing?
          I read a book
with holes punched in the pages. Upon
photocopying, the holes become black
squares, little wells of censor-toner.
I avoid the gaze of singular items.
I lament my floors.
          I carry with me
when I walk long distances
volumes of things which could have been.

To open the mouth is to experience pain

[The Sacrifice of Jephthah's Daughter, Pietro della Vecchia, ca. 1650]

Love's preoccupations transcend like the day
through water—bent, in need of definition. To imagine
an oath is to perform a calculation with only zeroes.
After all, the word weighs less than a seed husk,
reels on a cumulus puff
                      of breath.
                                    O, a balloon.
And the whisper-light of *th*, half a faith, half of this
whistling gesture across the throat. And yet—

O gravity's moan
O inexorable sigh of stone

                      What then, what then
of the latter hiss,
the phoebe flung from moistened lips, hollow-boned—

Wind your fingers through her hair. Make the mosaic
of what she holds for you grow wings, fly against all
you have sworn, make it sing. Some child,
some beautiful thing. What
                        kneels
                                before us, shouldering
against the brightness of the blade? Is it acceptance,
the shadowed pallor of your face?

The knife will know of all we fail to keep,
will rend in sameness any flesh.
Forgive the holder.   Forgive the rest.

She said *between* Part 3

Pronouns are both a problem
And a solution for Ashbery why

Hasn't anyone written that article
Yet why can I not lie down among
The fact that

On Tuesdays and Thursdays
I might actually be an *it*
Whereas on Sundays I am without
Fail eating oranges in the kitchen

Draped in lovely rumpled striped
Linen my feet doing something
Whose only correlative is *padding*

And isn't that something that girls
Do isn't that the texture of food
We know to be sweet and full of
Vitamins like C
              I am doing my part

Both to age more slowly and to
Internalize that clarity does not
Remedy suffering

And if you were to ask me how
To make space for an extra heart
In the corridors
              between our legs
I would say that our lives rise
And fall with the half tide of each
Murky estuary
              we hold under our
Protection:
        the heron's fixed eye,
The confusion of fish new to
This world and its expectations

The bass line to Ciaran Lavery's "A Ragtime Song" is almost identical to that of Ani DiFranco's "Pulse," she finds out at thirty-three

The latter of course being the song to which many forms of rocking happened, e.g. both of the back and forth and the more cranial variety, as well as discovery, for instance, of certain physical truths, to be more specific, that the lip and the earlobe have a similar give, that *hunger* is a bad metaphor for an overarching need to embrace, that one's first real sexual encounter rises up out of fumbled attempts to convince oneself that the round peg goes in the round hole very good A+, in reality, DiFranco's bass lines have always snaked beneath her lyrics like a toe sliding up the inner leg line, in this instance I look at the bug metaphor and I think *how am I supposed to write anything about the girl that I loved and hurt when it's already been done for me,* "all the rest of that bug stuff," artists like The Weeknd are now generally seen as the pinnacle of music you'd want to do it to, which is fine I guess if you're into super aggressive heterosexuality, but let's make a fucking playlist (get it) for the cautious, for the sweet scared probing and the breath sour with nerves, for the stereo in the age of the blobject, for Absolut ad collections, for the fact that *drunk* is, in fact, a very good metaphor for the vertigo induced by encountering yourself in her hands, in the dark, where even were anyone's hands, why is that the first memory to go, for my apology, which I have been performing for seventeen years, which I have drugged away with a *pharmakon* of inadequate maps, for my devotion to the dim image of that four-poster bed, which flew at me like something out of a Madeleine L'Engle story when Lavery's song came up on the radio, something about the ears, how they carry the shocked silence of a song whose chorus is everything you said you'd remember.

I'll try to be less attentive to the voices, she said

The unsung, the unsung—

[*Spring.*]

how the grass bristles without meaning to.
(Softness underfoot, I mean)

                    how the warm walls
of houses transcend   the windows form planes from which
the eyes dip into mirrored wells the seeing   the self
we are the product mostly of thrashing delirious, dead wild
the miniature things everywhere and their effort   all these
verticalities

how the constant arch of the neck in May
                          may well cut off blood
flow to the brain   in other words the obvious, love is madness
it is observed
that women are closer to the earth—
that the celestial substance, like the substance of the earth, is mutable—

[difficult, all the shades of green.]

                      Imagine a man. He sails through
the air's various levels and never comes to rest,
never creates anything but a thin sapling,

stiff and stupid. *Brutes and vegetables*   *his own smallness*

What he does not see coming: the furious ground   forced
the emerging insect
seeing the flesh of the man as food.

Four-four, or, it's possible we make music because we are herd animals

Coursing down the pavement
pinkly, I'm a platelet in the blood
of a patient whose problem might be
genetic, or a penchant for potato chips—
either way, let's talk about transitions, about this
desert of a desk, the words a supposed
dessert, a drop in a bucket of sugar-
water, filled, drained down, filled again.
Or don't. Perhaps doors are an issue
for me in particular, the snap of the latch
like the nagging sense after a nightmare
that you're not alone in your nest.
That nighttime, that wrong neighborly-ness,
that knife to the neck of the dawn.
The dread of companionship—
a gross comparison, perhaps, but good
enough for grasping that generally,
another groaning soul in the gulf between
you and your goals is going, probably,
to be something with erotic teeth.
When in the course of human coitus it
becomes necessary for one cunt to dissolve
the political cock which has connected
etc etc. A credo for convincing yourself
that you're a dish for one. One of these days
I'll relish slipping from street to studio,
the cotton hush. I'm a half-success already,
I can't type and cling to a lover's skin
simultaneously. There's nothing sexy
about involuntary asking. Instead:
a carving want to wake immortal,
written into the frame and woodwork,
washed from wonder (interrog.)
to wonder (n.). Anyway, the warning
is this: the apple's chewed to the core,
and my hands fly to my head
like there's a hammer in there, it hurts

like hell and I can hardly speak so
I hardly do, but honey, when it happens,
I want you to hear it, I've been so careful,
so measured for you.

So what if everything's planted in neat rows?

Inchoate, the interactions between our differing fleshes—
in the orchard, what drops is soft, post-red, the darkening—

[in the orb of summer, moving towards the end
                              of a continuum of sugars]

when the absence of novelty in my life causes me to revisit
disasters that nevertheless made me wet at the time, I consider
the weight of my loneliness

like a late tomato, sweet and part of a vicious family, the cruelty
of nightshade *sounding* like something you'd want to put in your
mouth—

                   or what do I know, anyway. To the gone-man-woman
in my brain, sliding down my front: Give me

a litany of what we'll do, the range of it, let there be clothing
on the line, a light, checked shirt in the branches. I return and return

to the apple trees because they are perfect, because they contain
every shape in balance, mottle the ground, provide the pattern

on a fawn's hide—
                   flat tender of leaf and petal, the gradual orb,
the roughness, the unyielding and multiple knots, oh, god,
everything—

I do not wish to valorize eroticism for its own sake. In Edvard
Munch's *Death and Life,* all the sperm is on fire—
                            trees of seed, the woman leaning

into a deep blue-black shadow of herself, eyes closed, warming up.

But don't you think we already have enough meteorology, she said

In rain, the forthcoming incident.
Hair in the thin stockings of semi-soluble what's left.
The mind's levers and the recording of
the conventionally beautiful—
organic forms, the tiny exhalations
of the rosebushes in the palace garden—

dark shutters fastened to a much lighter-colored plaster wall.
If it were butter yellow,
would we blame the air,
would we blame the engagement

and its wooden planks. In the event. In the brick of the book
on the table and the pages
which rest upon one another like capabilities,

the incessant hours alter what we perceive to be fog,
what we perceive as striation.

Who needs more thoughts
about the sky.

The lack which hovers beyond has already been theorized
as the moment before waking in which you think,
falsely, that a minor god has cradled your face

in his hands made of diamond and tulle.

She said *between* Part 4

[*Warp and weft.*]

Moving through the hours, the t-shirts on the line hold on to one kind of gray while releasing another. This transferal has both nothing and everything to do with the body, as is common when one is trying to avoid lyric trendiness. Everyone wants to respond with graciousness to the breeze; everyone wants to adapt to environmental changes particularly when those changes involve keeping your head down and becoming a square of fabric tucked neatly into a drawer. Last autumn I was convinced for a time that I could be at once a woman and free from gender. I was dismembered by a combination of multiple errors and wide swaths of cotton poplin in both tan and white. Folding myself over a length of twine, I said to myself *there are bigger problems in this world than whether or not your hair reaches the compressed wooden composite of the decking*. But waking in the middle of calling your own name into a forest spells out its own kind of doom. Which is mood; even now I cannot avoid shuttling back and forth across the word's scaffold. Do I do I do I do I. I, oh, die—as in, the holy chance, six-sided, that I will open my eyes to find myself elasticated and at peace.

Favor: cleaning out the garage

has its obvious symbolism, I suppose, but
the squirrels have taken over, and they're so literal,
the way their nests record various autumns
in every corner, my broom erasing them, no,
piling them together, a collapse of years and years
of squirrels, oh, this black plastic bag, how it collects
us, this isn't even my garage, it's your garage, I don't even
have a garage, the rectangle of my car hunched
up against the elements outside my apartment—
I'm shuffling around the pieces of a puzzle
and let me tell you, this is a difficult puzzle,
it's leaves and leaves and a girl's bike with a basket
that says "Heartbreaker" on the brake casing,
a giant iron relief of William Shakespeare, sporty hubcaps,
garden implements that are obviously part of a set
because of the identical green paint on their handles,
three boxes marked "philosophy" in Sharpie,
an off-white bit of scrap metal, a pallet,
and at least fourteen cans of paint but only
in about three different colors—
later we'll have too much wine, we won't have
showered and our hands will smudge the glasses
in the same way that my clavicles will end up
smudged from the bruising, the pressure
of your wrists insisting that I give like clay, that
I turn out soft after hefting all that lumber,
that I be also a good container into which
to put things. At the time, I thought *how excellent*
to be a bucket. Now I remember your fingers, heavy
with silver, only as trembling slightly from age—
they say that women discount their pain, that
2 is 4, but in truth, it's a matter of a richer inner life,
I was thinking about the garage door which
we fixed, which shut and stayed shut and did not
bounce back up because the last thing you did was
to install the motor improperly, it took some adjustments,
but now it moves smoothly, every press of the button
accompanied by a predictable slide, a landing
that sticks and makes it very difficult for anything
to destroy your possessions from the inside out.

I wanted to write about cooking, she said, but then I realized

Knife strokes to the parachute cords.
Intellection like a braid, learned, released
into conjured waves: after thinking, the mind
bobs differently in its clawfoot tub made of bone. Tall

windows and something bubbling
in a pot. They tell you to rub the skin
off of beets with a paper towel, but this
method is inexact unless you're looking to tie-

dye a lot of paper towels a lurid pink.
Which would be one way of calling for help—
I am about to use an ill-advised metaphor involving butter!
—but who would see it other than the woman on the

balcony across from you, the one
whose hair contrasts so starkly with
the crisp white of her shirt? Surely the wrought
iron in your life holds the designs you've made by

accident, while you were glowing
with fire. You pray for the return of lust
more concrete than the vaulted space between
you and the line of buttons, there, on the other side

of the street. She said my desire *for women
seems incompatible with the fact of everything else
in my life.* Little bars of papaya-scented soap near
the sink. Pots and pans, the way she watches carefully

as he takes the first forkful. Do not
mistake observation for tenderness. But you
know this—all the heart has gone out from your
stirring, you follow instructions, you go to bed and dream

of your own hands. The shape of
the woman in the white shirt slices across

the red root in your belly, snaps a sheet in the air
full of the low dove-sounds that mean perhaps never.

Sometimes, she thinks she prefers him on the other side of the screen

The jury

by which we mean the jury of scientists, in the court
of *figuring out how we stand each other—*

is out on the question of the precise nature
of the human relational form. Sure, there is no question
that we are herd and swarm, that we clump
together in terror and brandish flashlights uselessly
into the dark of ourselves—
                                          but no one

seems set on our preferences for really sharing air—

On the TV, we coo at the Laysan albatross as much
for the impossibility
of its head feathers, which disappear
into one another
and are beautiful for it

    as for its commitment to repetition, which we see as a virtue
        in all things.

When it grieves, it does so for one
or two years. When we are alone, we are expected

to tread the floors and to slip with open mouths through doorways.

What if I told you that even an arm's length wasn't enough?
What if I told you that I do not reconcile
                                  my desire for touch with
a preference, not unlike that of the albatross,
to spend the weighted balance of my life
wheeling, impossible wingspan, impossible
levity, over the singular platform of the sea?

Either pro or against Corinthians

[depending on whether or not you are in the audience at a wedding]

What in the Bible insinuates
The equivalence between the groom as groom
And the deity who gives and demands your personhood as charity

One has a choice

One hasn't a choice

In the overarching banality of marriage
Where do you go to find the definition of what you may or may not
Be doing in a given moment

I mean

Does forgiveness manifest itself in the dryer
Or is that patience

When we are told not to find God in the evening
Does that then imply that we are then to lie quiet

To recognize the absence
To recognize the kindness of the absence

Anyone that tells you they're in the business of providing answers
Has a garden of fist-sized cacti that they are drowning in speech.

For you, I would do nothing.

For you, I would push the Earth like a marble
Into the rope ring of the sun.

The thing that Trakl said about pain and thresholds
Is the real reason why the bride

Must be carried across

Into the room where she is all movement and all stillness.

There is nothing wrong with being transported
Only then

After all

Can another know why we make ourselves heavy on the ground
As a form of perseverance

NOTES

"To open the mouth is to experience pain": See the Book of Judges chapters 11-12; also, Bernard Aikema, "Pietro Della Vecchia, A Profile." *Saggi e Memorie di Storia dell'Arte* 14 (1984), 77-100, 171-206.

"If there were flight, I'd eliminate the snow": the book(s) referred to is/are Stephen King's *The Dark Tower* series, which are both awesome (in the literal sense) and problematic (as King often is when it comes to women).

"Either pro or against Corinthians": cf. Barbara Johnson, "Anthropomorphism in Lyric and Law." *Yale Journal of Law & the Humanities* 10.2 (1998). The Trakl poem referenced is "Winterabend."

"I'll try to be less attentive to the voices, she said": italics from Susan Griffin, *Woman and Nature: The Roaring Inside Her* (Berkeley, CA: Counterpoint, 1978).

Kimberly Quiogue Andrews received her MFA in creative writing from Penn State University and her PhD in English from Yale University. She is currently Assistant Professor of English and Creative Writing at Washington College in Chestertown, Maryland. She has garnered two Academy of American Poets prizes and a Pushcart Prize nomination for her poetry, and the Ralph Cohen Prize in criticism for her scholarship. Her recent work in various genres appears in *Poetry Northwest, The Shallow Ends, The Recluse, the Los Angeles Review of Books, ASAP/J,* and elsewhere. You can find her on Twitter at @kqandrews.

www.ingramcontent.com/pod-product-compliance
Lightning Source LLC
LaVergne TN
LVHW041600070426
835507LV00011B/1200